homespun

homespun

Cynthia Pappas

Copyright © 2017, Cynthia Pappas
All rights reserved.
Published in the United States of America
First Printing: 2017
ISBN 978-1-935516-01-9

"Dunhill's Maxim" was first published as "Friendship Gifts" in
    MaryJanesFarm in October-November 2016.
"Homemade" was first published as "Making Masterpieces" in
    Threads, a publication of the Taunton Press in September 2016.
"Accelerate. Focus. Explode." was first published in *Oregon
    Quarterly*, Spring 2000, and subsequently published in *Best
    Essays Northwest*, University of Oregon Press in 2003.
"Searching for My Father" was first published as "A Greek Odyssey"
    in *The Register-Guard* (Eugene, Oregon) in December 1998.
"Soil to Soul" was first published as "Get to Bed, You Carrot Tops" in
    Garden, Deck and Landscape, a Special Interest Publication of
    Better Homes and Gardens, in Spring 1998.
"Deluge" was first published as "Flood of 1996" in *The Register-
    Guard* (Eugene, Oregon) in April 1997.
"On Our Own" was first published as "Emotional Journey" in *The
    Register-Guard* (Eugene, Oregon) in September 1996.

Cover design by Sherri Van Ravenhorst

Coincidental
Communications

Published by
Coincidental Communications, LLC
P.O. Box 11511
Eugene, OR 97440

Note to Reader

The essays contained in this collection were written over the course of thirty years. Most were written in present tense, contemporaneously with the events being described. Some were written in past tense, long after the event occurred. These essays can be sampled individually in any order. However, the chronologically inclined will reap a homespun harvest by reading the chapters in the order they appear.

Contents

1   Diving Into Life

7   Homemade

11   Transplant

15   Deluge

23   On Our Own

27   Soil to Soul

31   Dunhill's Maxim

35   Church of Carson Hot Springs

39   Accelerate. Focus. Explode.

43   Reluctant Spirit in Training

49   Searching for My Father

55   No Time to Die

65   Hair Dating

69   Schooled by the Herd

75   What the Road Reveals

Diving into Life

I was born without a hip socket. Cursed with hip dysplasia like an inbred German Shepherd, I didn't walk until I was three years old. There are only a handful of full body photographs of me from when I was born in 1958 to when I finally had my last leg braces removed in 1961. In one of the pictures, my sister Sallie sits on the brown bouclé-upholstered chair in the living room holding me in her lap. We look like we are about one and three. I can't imagine the weight of my waist-to-toe body cast on her. In another photo, I perch in a child-size rattan chair with my legs splayed like a contortionist, wearing a brace with a big metal bar running from one foot to the other. Sallie stands next to me in our yard, in front of some newly planted birch trees. We wear Easter dresses that Mom made for us.

I have only one physical artifact left from that time—a wide, felted-wool belt, just fifteen inches around, with four hooks hanging from it, like a garter belt for a large doll. It must have been part of a harness worn around my waist or chest to hold my hips in alignment for the brace I wore when I finally "graduated" from a cast.

Fortunately, the doctors at Little Company of Mary Hospital in Torrance, California, diagnosed my hip dysplasia at an early checkup. They referred me to Long Beach Children's Hospital for treatment. The treatment at that time was to hold the hip stationary in a cast for some period to allow time for a socket to grow, and then rotate the femur and hip ball, and recast the hip. My leg was rotated one hundred and eighty degrees across a three-year span, like the Rockettes performing a low left-to-right kick on stage, but in extremely slow motion, with a body cast on. Rotation of my hip ball was supposed to cause the sacrum to form its own socket; thus there would be no need for grafting, nor an artificial hip. It was a success.

In 1959, Dad secured a new job at Litton Industries in Woodland Hills, so we moved from Long Beach to the San Fernando Valley. He had top secret clearance to work on the navigation systems for F-15 fighter jets. With no orthopedic specialists in the Valley, Mom had to drive me to the Long Beach Children's Hospital, as far from the San Fernando Valley as Mars. It took all day. Getting there in the pre-freeway era meant spending an eternity on old Sepulveda Road. I don't know if my mom always hated driving or if she hated driving after having to make this trip too many times. I do know that she would go to ridiculous lengths to avoid making a left turn against oncoming traffic.

As each rotation of my hip was completed, the doctor would remove the cast with a saw, rotate my leg into another contorted position, and plaster on yet another cast. It's no wonder that I have no recollection of any of this, except for the scant information my mom shared with me when she felt I needed to know. My mom and dad must have worried constantly, fearing that the treatment might not work, and that I would have to navigate the rest of my life with a permanent limp or in a wheelchair.

Mom did tell me that I was a terror in the house, that I would drag myself around on my hands, clumping my heavy, wide cast behind me.

By the time I was born, my dad had already spent years dealing with his own disability: complete deafness in one ear and partial deafness in the other, the result of a debilitating case of the measles when he was a child. He wore hearing aids as big as Brussels sprouts. To accommodate his difficulty with hearing, we became a loud-talking family. I thought it was normal to carry on conversations in my "outdoor voice." Dad's condition kept him from fighting in World War II—a blessing because he lived through the war when so many didn't, but also a curse because it made him different. Being different was not a good thing in the conformist 1950s.

I can imagine my dad thinking, "I don't want people's pity when they look at Cindy, so we'll only take her out of the house if we have to." My mom once told my sister about an incident in a grocery store. As we shopped, my dad carried me in my cast. My dad was a slight man—five-foot-eight and one hundred forty-eight pounds—so I must have been a heavy load. A lady in the checkout line said, "What a cute baby. But is she all right in the head?"

Once I got the last braces off, I never stopped moving. I figure I had a lot of catching up to do. I am a doer—I walk fast, I think fast, I eat fast. And if I can do more than one thing at a time, all the better. I don't want to lead a lop-sided life by focusing too much on one thing.

The only admonitions I received growing up centered around being proud of how you carry yourself in the world: "Shoulders back, don't slouch." "Pick up your feet when you walk." And, as a subtle reminder to always give it your all, Mom would preach: "all you can do is the best you can do."

I knew from an early age that I wanted to be the captain of my own ship. At five, I started "Cindy's Ballet of School." Although Sallie tried to convince me that I had the words in the wrong order and it should be Cindy's School of Ballet, I was stubborn and refused to reorder the words to her liking. I had to do it my way. The only student was Cheryl, the girl who lived across the street. The main lesson involved jeté-ing across the front lawn, trailing one of my mom's scarves.

Sallie, two years older than me, had appointed herself my corrector and protector. When I was running barefoot on the lawn and stepped on a bee, she scooped me up in her arms and ran me into the house so Mom could pull out the stinger. When I cut my head on the filigreed wood of the window boxes during a game of hide-and-seek, and the blood coursed down my cheeks, Sallie scooped me up and carried me into the bathroom so Mom could clean the blood off and see whether stitches were required. This was all well and good, but it forever created this dynamic of the good sister who doesn't take risks versus the sister who never thinks twice and dives into life. Subtle as a freight train is what my mom used to say about me. My sister refers to my life as the "Flight of the Bumble Bee."

Every day my dad would drive home from work for lunch. I never understood whether this was a way of saving money or if he was too shy to eat with his coworkers. He was a man of few words. During the summer, without the schedule of school to impede my business pursuits, I eagerly anticipated his arrival. I would ask Dad what he wanted to order for lunch. Order pad in hand, I would list the choices—tuna fish sandwich or peanut butter and jelly sandwich—and wait for his reply. I prepared his sandwich and served it to him. When he finished he would leave me a dime tip. Those dimes were like gold to me.

In July, Mom would pack the camper in anticipation of Dad's vacation, and we'd head off to the Sierras. Sallie and I would bring our Barbie dolls and make camp for them. They never had the right outfits for camping and would continually lose their pumps in the pine duff.

Dad taught us how to fish for trout. He said, "Hold the rod and swing it back to two o'clock, then forward to ten o'clock and release the line." If the bobber on the line was pulled underwater, it was time to gently reel in your fish. Mom would panfry the trout for dinner after coating it in flour, salt, and pepper.

One time we caught too many fish to eat, so we left some in a bucket of lake water overnight. We had visitors to our camp that night. Raccoons ate the fish, then proceeded to climb up the picnic table and open a Tupperware container of my favorite dessert—date bars—and eat every last one of them. The next morning, our picnic table was covered with paw prints of sticky dates and stinky fish.

Everything seemed to come easy to me. I got straight A's in school. I had an overabundance of empathy to share.

I bonded with my teachers. I was well-liked by most. Loners gravitated to me—like Mimi, the girl with the club foot, and painfully shy Kelly.

The only person I had trouble with was Peggy, the bully, an unhappy girl who thought I was weird for hanging out with misfits and overachievers. Bullies don't like smart girls. In sixth grade, Peggy, with her entourage of hangers-on, challenged me to a fight: "meet me at the poles." The poles existed somewhere outside Enadia Way Elementary School, far enough from the school ground that teachers couldn't see the action. Scared, and picturing myself bruised and bloodied, I went to the principal, Mrs. Peoples, and told on Peggy. I don't recall the outcome for Peggy, but I do know that we never met at the poles.

In spite of spending my first three years in braces and a cast, I have always felt lucky; I was born to parents who cared deeply about raising their children with the trinity of homework, chores, and play. We understood that education was paramount, work was important, and play came last. This is the ethic I internalized as a kid and can't unlearn.

I am deeply grounded by my parents' belief in me and unwavering support of my mercurial ambitions. They never extinguished my fire. I was encouraged to dive in as long as there was no risk of bodily injury. When I said I wanted to be the next Linda Ronstadt, Mom would always tell me how much she loved to hear me sing. When I set a goal of earning all thirty-four Girl Scout badges, Mom patiently sewed each one of them onto my green sash.

Mom showed me that "hard work is its own reward" as she religiously tended her gorgeous flower garden and canned summer peaches so we could enjoy their sweetness in the dark of winter. I am thankful, looking back on all the simple things my parents did and didn't do, said and didn't say, that freed me to be myself and not some watered-down version of a girl.

homespun

Homemade

I spent my growing-up years watching my mom sew. I loved the metallic smell of buttons in her tin button box. I would open the blue tin box to scoop up handfuls of buttons she had snipped off clothes that were worn out or outgrown. Once I asked my mom about a set of buttons she had strung together with twine. The size of fifty-cent pieces, they were bluish gray. "Oh, those were on my wedding suit," she informed me. Every button had a history that she could recite.

We were a do-it-yourself family based on necessity rather than choice. We had a DIY lifestyle long before that concept became a way of showing your hipster chops. I sometimes envied the girls who wore store-bought dresses to school. But I knew the formula—one yard for a miniskirt; two yards to make a pair of pants. A shirt required one-and-a-half yards.

Our Halloween outfits were always homemade, sewn by Mom. The creations began with a trip to the Home Silk Shop—the Cadillac of fabric stores. I would head first to the tables loaded with pattern books—McCall's, Butterick and Vogue—and turn to the section for costumes. But they never had patterns that matched my dreams. Instead, we searched for material to create something unique. In third grade, Sallie and I became Kato and the Green Hornet, from the TV show. That year, we came home with three yards of black faux leather.

Out of this slick, shiny-as-rain-on-pavement fabric, Mom fashioned a beret with a jacket to match. I wore black tights and a black turtleneck. Sallie and I spent most of October fake karate chopping each other; yelling "Ha!" I remember racing down the dark hall trying to elude Sallie's chop and running into the bathroom for a quick escape. I leapt onto the toilet lid to position myself for a surprise attack, only to find someone had left the lid up. I splashed right into the cold water.

In fourth grade, I was Jeannie from the TV show *I Dream of Jeannie.* Mom made me pink satin harem pants with a bolero to match, and a white silky blouse with puffed sleeves. Mom pulled back every blond hair on my ten-year-old head into a high ponytail until my eyebrows felt tight. My ponytail cascaded straight out of the pink headpiece that she made and bobby-pinned to my hair. I kept pressing my palms together and blinking my eyes just like Jeannie so everyone could get the full effect. Sallie was a flapper wearing a shiny red satin dress with rows of swingy, silky black fringe and fishnet stockings.

For every special occasion, Mom would create a special outfit. For Sallie's sixth-grade graduation, Mom made a turquoise-blue sleeveless dress with a swath of vertical white lace centered down the front, topped by a lace bow—*exactly* like the outfit worn by Barbie's sister, Skipper. Every Easter Mom made us new dresses. One year we went to see the swallows return to Mission San Juan Capistrano, and Mom made me a dress of white cotton fabric with a brown print. The empire-waist dress was tied with a bow made from brown velvet ribbon. New white patent leather shoes and white lace anklets completed the outfit.

When it was time to cut out the fabric, Mom would spread her cutting board out on the living room floor. It was the only place in our tiny ranch home big enough to unfold three yards of material.

She sewed our clothes during commercial breaks at night while my dad watched TV. She couldn't sew during the shows because it made fuzzy lines on the television screen and then Daddy couldn't see his football or basketball game. It took a *lot* of commercials to finish one outfit.

She stationed herself in the green chair in the corner of the living room with the best light for doing handwork and then raced into the bedroom to sew a seam. Timing was critical. Sallie and I would yell, "Show's back on!" and she came back out to the living room to baste the next seam.

We never got through a holiday without an outfit hemmed at the last minute, including my wedding dress! It required standing on a chair in the kitchen, holding the box of pins, while Mom leaned the yardstick up against my legs and pinned the hemline. "Turn. Other way. Okay, now back. There. Now, be careful of the pins when you take it off."

Mom believed that homemade was a statement of originality, rather than an apology for not being able to afford store-bought. She always said, "No one else will have an outfit just like yours." I wish I had saved some of those dresses with the careful French seams: my prom dress with the marabou-edged shrug, the lime green and purple bathing suit, or the camel hair coat lined with satin. They were masterpieces.

Mom continues to influence my life even though she passed ten years ago. When I sew, I feel her steadying hands, encouraging patience.

Transplant

I left my southern California Valley Girl days behind in 1980 to attend graduate school in Oregon. After earning my master's degree, I found a job with a regional planning agency working on a long-range urbanization plan for the Eugene-Springfield area. My job involved contentious meetings with the public and elected and appointed officials, where I described what areas were planned for future city growth and what areas would be preserved as farm and forest land. At one meeting of the Lane County Planning Commission, a really cute commissioner with sandy brown hair that fell onto his forehead asked a lot of seriously smart questions. Smart is my favorite aphrodisiac.

After a little sleuthing, I found out his name was George and he wasn't married. As told to me by a mutual acquaintance, George wondered, "Who's that cute staffer who gives smart answers?" He found out I was single and asked me out. I was all "c'mon let's go!" George, an analyzer, wasn't as quick to jump at the idea of marrying again. Eventually I wore him down. Along with the marriage came two stepsons, a farm, two dogs, a commercial raspberry operation, and, it turns out, a whole new education.

I had no qualms about the move to a sixty-six-acre spread in east Springfield. What could be so complicated about taking care of a barn, a shop (not a garage), and a huge farmhouse? After all, I grew up in Los Angeles. I could handle anything—like rush-hour traffic on the 405 Freeway and finding a parking space at the mall. This cockiness did not serve me well on the farm.

One day while playing a board game called Farm Game with George and the boys, I test my newfound knowledge about crops.

"I just lost my wheat field."

"No Cindy, that's your second cutting of hay you just lost," Nat, the oldest, informs me, ever the one to be precise about things.

"Wheat, hay, what's the difference?" I quip, quickly passing the dice to their father to distract them from my ignorance. This transplant needs more time to develop roots.

I move onto the farm in early July, at the height of raspberry season. The phone constantly rings. Workers show up far too early in the morning to start picking. The row boss gets them organized. Last-minute emergencies have to be dealt with before I leave for work and before George drives the boys into town for school. Folks call to ask if we have U-pick. This is a new term to this city girl. In Springfield, farmers offer U-pick raspberries, pumpkins, blueberries, apples, pears, cherries, and strawberries. You could spend the entire summer U-picking.

One night, one of our neighbor's cows gets out. Some evenings the cows go for a neighborhood stroll. We have searched for the weak spot in the fence between our neighbor's pasture and ours to no avail. Returning home after dark from a City Council meeting, I almost run into a cow as I drive up our half-mile-long gravel driveway. She is mooing loudly. As I maneuver the car around the cow, my headlights arc across the front of the house. I see my husband hanging his head out of our second-story bedroom window. I stop the car.

He yells out to me, "Hey Hon, since you still have your shoes on, could you get the cow back into the neighbor's pasture? She's been bellowing and I know she's thirsty."

How long can this have been going on, I wonder, if he's had time to figure out that the darn cow needs water? Being a good farm wife, I hop out of the car in my high heels and suit and start walking slowly toward the cow. Cows look much bigger up close than when you see them standing out in a field.

"Shoo! Yaw! Get in there ... go on..." I say firmly to the cow. I choose words that usually make animals move, or at the very least pay attention. Nothing doing.

George, laughing hysterically by now, yells "grab a stick and hit it on the butt." I find a branch on the ground, but I'm not about to get close enough to the cow to reach her fanny. I whack the stick on the ground and repeat my verbal prodding. The cow never even looks up.

Why can't the cow figure out how to get back in if it's smart enough to get out? The stand-off ends when George acquiesces to putting his boots on and coming outside. With one strong whack and a loud "Yaw!" he gets the cow back into the neighbor's pasture.

Living on this farm, I learn to share my life with a lot more than wandering cows. We have a bee colony living under the eaves, and the dogs catch gophers and then want to play fetch, using the gopher as a "stick." I disagree with John Denver's portrayal of farm life as "kind of laid back." We must constantly and vigilantly search for moles in the garden, mice in the laundry room, and starlings that accidently come down the chimney into the living room. As a fifth-generation farmer, my husband takes all this in stride.

One day I come home from work to an empty house and hear an odd sound in the living room, like a deck of cards being shuffled. It seems to be emanating from the chimney. There are ashes fanning out from the fireplace onto the wood floor. As I approach, the sound becomes more frantic. It's a bird caught in the chimney. I open the flue and out he flies, landing on the back of a chair, eyeing me nervously. He proceeds to poop on the chair and then crashes into the window, trying to escape. I run up the stairs to Josh's room and grab his butterfly net and trap the terrified bird. I take it outside and release it, hoping it won't make the same mistake twice.

Being conversant with the country way of life is a challenging experience. My attempts to master a bewildering array of farm equipment remain a work in progress. The tractor, baler, and rototiller all require different mixes of gasoline, different starting procedures and a lot of elbow grease. When I am at wit's end, I remind my husband that there is a reason all this machinery is referred to as "implements of husbandry."

Since moving to the farm, I notice a ritual that almost everyone I meet seems to observe. They buy seeds, rototill their lawn (a sacrilege in LA), and plant a garden. The novel idea of planting seeds to grow food that will last you through the winter leads me to secretly feel that I have moved into a neighborhood of survivalists. At harvest time, this ritual continues with canning the fruits of the garden. The ritual comes full circle at the holidays when friends share their produce with each other as gifts. Pretty nifty, actually, even though it takes some getting used to.

Living on this farm has given me a sense of neighborliness I couldn't have imagined in LA. We exchange zucchini for sunflower bouquets, and salsa for use of the extension ladder. We help each other cut and stack hay in late June. When the power goes out, whoever has a generator invites the others over to watch TV in a warm house. We share the rhythm of the seasons and feel extraordinarily blessed to live along the McKenzie River.

This transplant has started to set down deep roots already. I thrive on being in touch with the land, and bloom from the love of a ready-made family.

Deluge

What started as typical February showers transformed into curtains of pounding, eroding rain. Eight inches of rain combined with sixty-degree temperatures caused all the snow below 3,000 feet to melt.

I arrived home at 10 p.m. from writing class. As soon as I got out of the car, I could hear the normally placid water of Cedar Creek surging past our farmhouse. George met me in the kitchen, saying "It's coming up fast." I grabbed a flashlight, went back outside, found a stick, and stuck it in the mud to mark the water level. Five feet to go before the creek would top its banks. A first-time experience for me, living on this farm.

George and I fell into an uneasy sleep while the rain sheeted and the creek rose.

At 2:30 a.m. we both lay wide awake. A subtle shift in noise level, perhaps? We dressed quickly and headed out to get a visual reading on the creek. I approached with my flashlight and stopped abruptly; the marker had vanished, completely submerged.

A foot more and Cedar Creek would rise to the top of the bank. We jumped in the car to see whether our driveway that runs parallel to the creek had been breached. We drove out to Sixty-sixth Street to find out if it was still passable. Both our driveway and the street had only normal puddles so far. But as we drove slowly along Thurston Road, we occasionally angled the car so our headlights would light up the field and everywhere, in all directions, the reflection of our headlights danced off water.

After a fifteen-minute inspection, we turned back down Sixty-sixth toward the McKenzie River. In that short amount of time, Cedar Creek had breached the bank and now flowed across the road. We didn't talk much in the car, each of us lost in our own thoughts.

As we approached our driveway, we saw neighbors J.C. and Della in their barn where they stood in water a foot deep already. As they moved things up off the floor, we spoke briefly, trying to get a sense of how fast the water was rising. Tension punctuated our sentences. Back at home we were greeted by our two German shorthaired pointers, Lucy and Nanook, both awake at the odd hour, sensing something wrong. After reassuring them, we staggered back to bed, foolishly thinking we might capture a few more hours of sleep before moving into high gear.

Thirty minutes later, our neighbor Bill drove his truck down our driveway to check on us. Clearly, we could not go back to sleep now. The creek topped its banks at 4 a.m. and kept rising. We scanned our flashlights over the ground and into the shop.

Water already oozed through the joint between the shop foundation and walls. By 7 a.m. we had moved everything off the shop floor onto the uneasy protection of sawhorses covered with sheets of plywood.

The water moved violently, noisily, all around us: surging over the rock wall next to the shop, cutting away under the concrete pad we had laid just a year ago, rolling across our perennial bed, transforming our yard into a smaller and smaller refuge.

By first light, the creek had fully breached the berm along our half-mile-long driveway, cutting off our house from the road. Turbid water poured across the driveway, scouring the rock bed and moving truckloads of gravel into our neighbor's pasture.

I called my mom, describing the situation but reassuring her in a wavering voice that we were OK. Startled at the early morning call, she said she didn't realize things were so bad, and she would start worrying right away.

Only seven miles separated our two houses, yet she had no idea of the flood's magnitude. I agreed that if any circumstance warranted the famous Pappas worrying machine, this was probably it.

Another neighbor, Dagmar, called to ask if we could make it across our field to her barn to feed her horses. The rising waters of the McKenzie River had cut her house off from her horse barn. George put on his fly-fishing waders and boots and set out across the north pasture. I watched him through the binoculars to make sure I didn't lose sight of him as he made his way slowly through thigh-high water.

A couple of hours later, neighbor Mary rowed across our field in her drift boat. Another creek that flows across our north property line had risen to combine with the McKenzie, providing passageway for her boat. After she rowed up to our back deck and tied off, she told us she was searching for four missing cows. We hadn't seen them. Mary couldn't make it back to her place rowing against the current, so I loaned her my waders and boots and she set off across the pasture toward her farm, with me watching to make sure she made it safely through the field.

Even though the house sits on a three-and-a-half-foot-high foundation, George and I decided to move everything from the first floor of the house to the second floor. The *fwap-fwap-fwap* sound of a helicopter evacuating neighbors punctuated our heaving breaths. It took us only thirty minutes as adrenalin swamped our bodies.

By noon, raging whitewater surrounded the house. The water swirled around the third of four porch stairs. Sixty-sixth Street had become completely impassable. At midday the phone rang. The Springfield Fire and Life Safety crew stationed on Thurston Road said we should evacuate immediately. The helicopter was on its way.

Unfortunately, after slogging around in the mucky water and moving furniture, I had picked that very moment to take a shower. I knew the high water could shut our pump down soon and leave us without running water.

Midway though my shower I heard George's voice magnified by the empty living room, "Get out of the shower *right now*. We need to be ready to go!"

My heart pounded as I hurriedly struggled to dress, launching myself down the stairs two at a time. "What's going on?" I asked George.

"The helicopter is on a schedule and we're next in line!"

We received a second phone call from the Fire and Life Safety crew after they realized they had no dry place to land near our home. So we locked the house, loaded the dogs and two backpacks into the drift boat that Mary left tied to our deck, and pushed off. No time to think about what we'd left behind.

George rowed down our driveway against the current, in Class II whitewater, through our neighbor Bill's pasture, over heavily listing barbed wire fence, past cows huddled on a tiny patch of high ground. A couple of times when the boat got stuck, we had to get out and pull the boat over the low spots.

The helicopter overhead marked our passage through the pasture. We left the drift boat tied up near Bill's barn. With our packs on our backs, we inched along the fence line through four-foot-deep water that rushed across Sixty-sixth Street. George walked in front of me, carrying sixty-five-pound Nanook in both arms. A firefighter carried Lucy. I wrapped my left hand around a fence rail to stay upright. At one point it looked like the strength of the current was going to sweep George under. Clearheaded and detached in the face of appalling jeopardy, I pushed his right shoulder against the current, toward the railing, to keep him upright.

Reaching the safety of high ground, I looked up, having focused all morning on water beneath me and around me. Neighbors lined the road, their faces etched with concern, wondering if they, too, would eventually have to evacuate. Still, they shared encouraging words and welcoming hugs. My adrenalin melted into tears.

We spent the night at my mom's house in Eugene,

drying wet clothes, dealing with phone calls from panicked neighbors who had to leave their horses behind. As I lay in bed, the sound of Cedar Creek pulsed and raged in my ears.

When I went to work the next morning, George returned to the farm to survey the damage, not knowing if our home would be full of mud. He called to tell me that the water came within inches of flowing through our house. The wall of our walk-in cooler (that we used to store freshly picked raspberries for our berry operation) blew out from the force of the swollen creek. Our access road, scoured by churning water and rocks, required our four-wheel drive to navigate. A high waterline marked the siding of our shop, and inches of muck and mud coated the floor inside. Gravel from the pathway around the house lay in piles on the lawn, like tiny glacial moraines.

In stark contrast, for work that evening I had to attend an opening reception for the major donors of the Historic Springfield Interpretive Center, the culmination of a multi-year planning effort. When we evacuated, the only clothing I thought to pack in my backpack was the outfit I would wear to the event: a black velvet dress, patent leather heels, and pearls. I had made the mental leap to Thursday night's event, but had not thought about what I would be left to wear all day at work: rubber boots and filthy jeans.

The next day, my sister called me at work, reporting that our dog Lucy had disappeared. We had left our dogs at my mom's house until the high water receded and we could get our driveway reconstructed. My heart dulled to a new low. We printed flyers and handed them out at the businesses near my mom's house, talked with all the neighbors, gave out our phone number, and prayed someone would see her and contact us. And we searched. We felt totally deflated, having come through the flood only to lose Lucy.

Operating on sleep deprivation and very sore muscles, we invited a crew of friends over to help us clean the mud out of the shop and move gravel.

The following night we got a call telling us that someone had spotted Lucy on Beltline Highway near Coburg Road. George and I jumped into the car and raced over to north Eugene with our flashlights and doggie bones. We combed the median strips for half an hour, calling her name.

Then we saw her, tucked back-end into a blackberry thicket. She came when we called, rolled over on her back, and wagged her tail. Lucy, George, and I shared our incredible joy and relief. Safely back in the car, she sat on my lap and I hugged her all the way home. Our wayward pup ate ravenously at home, then slept twelve hours straight.

With Lucy back, we felt like a family again. Watching TV that evening, I heard a loud *thunk* in the laundry room, where our thirteen-year-old dog, Nanook, was sleeping off his dinner. Having been on high alert for the better part of six days at this point, I jumped up from the couch to check on Nanook, who lay on his side with all four legs twitching uncontrollably. I held him tight and murmured reassurances.

Nanook's equilibrium was out of whack and he couldn't stand. His entire right side looked off kilter. George and I were concerned that the trauma of evacuation had been too much for the old boy. We got him back on his bed, made him comfortable, and resigned ourselves to another sleepless night.

Early the next morning I lifted Nanook into the car and arrived at the veterinarian's office when it opened. I left him to have some tests run. Ironically, the vet said Nanook needed to be rehydrated. When I picked him up that afternoon, he was weak and tottery on his feet.

Meantime, our well had not functioned for six days. When George finally turned on the pump switch, the wiring short-circuited from having been under water for too many days. A repair man from the local pump company pulled it out of its casing and rewired the switch. Then we had to chlorinate the water and wait before we could safely use the water faucets at home.

The following morning, George and my stepson Nat left on a flight to the East Coast for a father-son trip they had planned months ago to visit MIT and Princeton, so Nat could make his final decision about college.

I called FEMA (the Federal Emergency Management Administration) to report our flood damage, scheduled a visit with a flood inspector, talked with our insurance agent, got more bottled water from my sister, and checked in with all the neighbors. Too many days in row of uncertainty left me feeling emotionally shaken. I got teary-eyed talking to a friend as I showed her photos we had taken of the flood. My mind swam with thoughts of the many ways things could have ended up so much worse.

Three days after I called, the FEMA inspector pulled up to the house in her compact white car. I stepped outside to greet her. Right on time and full of purpose, she began peppering me with questions the minute she stepped out of the car.

"Where is your electric meter?" We walked toward the meter.

"What percentage of your driveway was left unusable?"

"How many cubic yards of gravel were required to bring your road back to standard where an emergency vehicle could safely gain access?"

"Did you have to replace or repair the wiring to get your pump working again?"

"What percentage of insulation in your crawl space got damaged?"

I had not assessed the damage in a way that FEMA found relevant. I could answer the questions about how long it took to rebuild the driveway and how long we were without water. By the time she left, I felt empty. We communicated on two very different levels.

Thank goodness our house remained intact. Nanook survived, but with diminished mobility. Mary's cows made it to high ground until the water receded. Dagmar's horses stood in three feet of water for most of one day, but came out unscathed. Bill's cow made it to his barn and gave birth to a calf the night of the flood. Piles of gravel dot the landscape, deposited where the current eddied or shifted. Still ahead was the enormity of the cleanup.

With George and Nat away, Lucy and Nanook shadowed me all weekend, unwilling to let me out of their sight, vigilant to any unusual sounds and smells. We walked the fence lines, picking up plastic pots from the potting shed, wooden trellises from the herb garden, lawn chairs that had been stored in the shop, a red ice chest. Lucy barked at familiar objects lodged in unfamiliar places. It was slow going as I sunk three inches into the mud with every step.

For weeks, well-intentioned people kept asking if things felt back to normal. Normal is ephemeral. The creek proved that to us whenever we stopped to listen. The water-weary ground was slow to recover. As were we.

On Our Own

It is the last night before my stepson, Nat, leaves for his freshman year at college. George and I invite Nat and his sweetheart to go for a walk as the evening light turns murky. This walk to inspect the fence we built is an excuse to have a moment together, to prolong the evening. Somehow I know when the walk is over, our pattern of time with Nat as we now experience it also will end. He will return at Christmas, broadened in ways that George and I both anticipate but can't articulate.

I have floundered anchorless through these past couple of weeks. Nat has been a significant part of my life for the past ten years. I have watched him grow from camper to camp counselor. From student to scholar. Seen his edges solidify into a strong core.

I also miss Josh, my other stepson, who two years ago decided to live with his mom full time and has only sporadically communicated with George and me since. Our family seems diminished. With both boys gone, I feel a profound sense of loss.

Over the past two months, I've been conscious of backing away from shared moments to allow time for George and Nat to connect. I know how hard this is on George. He has invested eighteen years of energy, anxiety, and love in raising Nat. In a rare moment of vulnerability, George remarked that not only would he be losing a son to the East Coast, but he'd be missing a friend as well.

Morning is here. The time to say goodbye has arrived.

The change in weather from days of intense sun to low clouds mirrors my mood. It is early, not my best hour. I feel fragile and depleted. Did I spend enough time involving myself in Nat's life? Has he packed enough clothes? Does he know how to balance a checkbook? Will he be carried buoyant through those rough homesick days by the knowledge of how much I love him?

I am mute at a time when I want so much to communicate. We mark the moment on film: Nat and his dad on the porch, George's face softened with love. Nat and I on the porch holding tightly to each other. Our two German shorthaired pointers, wriggling Lucy and arthritic Nanook, nudge Nat's hands, wanting attention and acknowledgment. The dogs know something is not quite right. Lucy keeps licking Nat's face—the universal dog language of comfort. Nat's stepfather arrives to share the long drive to Boston. One last picture of the van heading away down the driveway. I remember myself at Nat's age thinking the world was opening before me.

George and I spend the remainder of the morning wandering aimlessly through the house. I release my breath, as though I've been holding a balloon and have let it loose and watched it soar until even the tiny speck of color has disappeared. I am unsure how to absorb this transition of his, of ours.

I wait for my high school friend Teri to call. She and her family will visit on their way home from the Oregon coast. I welcome the distraction, a gift. We learn that they will arrive in time for dinner. Emotionally drained, George and I fall into a restless nap. Later I leave for the grocery store.

I return to find our hundred-year-old walnut tree has fallen across the driveway, narrowly missing the house. The demise of the massive tree starkly exposes the west side of our house. The walnut's branches lie heavy on the young lilac and red oak trees planted only a few years ago, bending them almost to the ground.

We must deal with the situation immediately. Perhaps there will be time later to sit with George and mourn Nat's leaving. George starts up the chain saw, amplifying my feeling of sadness. I am not ready to dismantle the old tree. I stand witness as George works the blade through the seasoned trunk and the young trees right themselves.

Soil to Soul

With no kids left at home to parent, George and I focus our inexhaustible supply of energy on our garden. Maybe a few extra plants might help fill the emotional void. We decide to raise tomatillos from seed, and indulge the gophers by planting enough potatoes so they can share in the harvest and we'll still have extras to drop off at the local food bank. This year we'll enter our eggplant at the Lane County Fair. With undivided attention, our pickling cucumbers will be transformed into prize-winning dills. With the Exhibitor's Handbook as our Doctor Spock, we can be the proud parents of "specimens true to type; deep in color; and uniform in size, shape, and texture."

"This garden just keeps growing," my husband jokes to me, as he unbends from planting the fourth row of tomato plants. I recite their names. Like a litany they roll off my tongue: Early Girl, Romas, Oregon Spring, Supersweet 100s. The green-earth fragrance of the tomato plants reminds me of the smell of a child emerging fresh from the shower.

On the darkest, wettest day in February, my husband and I find ourselves at the local hardware store searching for something to lighten the impermeable gray. I wonder how Nat is doing back at college. He was home for such a short time on holiday break. My husband calls from the next aisle, excited. "Seed packets are half price!" We buy handfuls of herb, flower, and vegetable seeds. I envision row upon garden row of bright fuschia-colored zinnia, tangerine nasturtium, and dandelion-yellow sunflowers intermixed with the deep greens of spinach and potato leaves, with the delicate filigree of dill towering over it all.

In late March, we have the first part of the garden planted with peas, lettuce, spinach, and arugula. In early April, we set about methodically installing broccoli and onions. This year we attempt some exotic potato varieties including Yellow Finn, Nooksack, Kennebec, and Russian fingerling. The following weekend we add rows of snap peas and sugar pod peas, bush beans, and beets. A week later the makings for Mexican feasts—cilantro, three varieties of peppers, and shallots—line up alongside rows of Chief and Torpedo corn. The vegetable garden expands to the size of a city lot to accommodate carefully sown flowers: bachelor's buttons, sweet peas, stock, and nasturtiums.

Weekends that get too soggy to garden, we plant black walnut trees along the property lines, replacing what we lost in the flood. After cleaning out the gravel from our footpath that was displaced in the flood, we buy a truckload of shrubs at our friend's nursery to plant under the birches. I fill terra-cotta pots with verbena, geraniums, petunias, and violets. The deck now spills with a riot of red, purple, and yellow blossoms that the hummingbirds can't resist. Bumblebees charge the tubular bells of foxglove gracing the entryway. Red-breasted sapsuckers *scree* as they methodically flit among the birch trees. The osprey chirp overhead and mallards tuck themselves into the brush lining the creek. As I hoe in the garden, a ring-necked pheasant peers out from the tall grass, trumpeting its hoarse, nasal call. Despite this cornucopia of splendor, I miss the sound of the boys' laughter and inquiries of "I'm starved. When's dinner?"

In the evening our ritual is to shed the eight-to-five work clothes, put on dusty shorts and shirt, grab the hoe and head for the garden. Two hours of care each night—planting, watering, hand weeding, and hoeing—substitute for correcting homework, offering advice, and attending band performances.

As I weed, my thoughts turn away from this gardening experience to a former one. Raising teens, you have to approach your objective obliquely for fear they might bolt. You plant the seed by offering something they can almost see out of the corner of their eye and then be on alert for that two-minute opportunity when they generously hold still and allow a hug. This new garden allows a more direct approach for our daily ministrations.

With each turning of the soil, I unearth more thoughts of our changed lives. We intended a smaller garden with the boys gone. But we have become consummate nurturers, their father and I. A vegetable garden cannot accommodate all our displaced love and attention. It has spilled over into a perennial garden filled with strawberries, asparagus, artichokes, blueberries, and raspberries.

There is no stopping us now. We map out a pumpkin patch to entice our nephews to visit. The scarecrow, stuffed with hay from the barn, stands sentinel at the corner post, beckoning them to enter and explore. Sunflowers, ornamental corn, and the orange globes of Big Max and Hybrid Autumn Gold fill the far corner of the garden.

I stand on the bedroom balcony gazing down on the garden like a proud parent, embracing its goodness with my eyes. Rich river-bottom loam peeks out between each row of green. Soon the plants will fill out. I have to pay close attention or I'll miss a stage of growth. The first true leaves on the Blue Lake beans appear overnight.

"We have broccoli heads already!" my husband calls out after a morning walk through the garden. It reminds me of the night we were reading the boys to sleep and Josh decided he would read the story to us instead. Or that brief period of time when Nat wore the same size shoes as me. It all happens so quickly.

I revel in the tiny white blossoms on the potato plants; they remind me of baby teeth. The peas are getting so leggy, they've almost outgrown their support, like bare ankles peeking out from too-short pants. My garden, my sons. Growing so fast.

Dunhill's Maxim

Friends are the gifts we hold in our hearts all year long. Making presents for the people we care about creates a deeply satisfying focus for our family to come together in a conscious act that allows us to more readily appreciate blessings that can't be bought.

In 1997 George and I decide to make cloth napkins and wooden napkin rings. We'll use pieces cut from the old walnut tree that toppled the day my oldest son left for college. I can already smell the wood shavings as George carefully cuts the wood into round shapes. He'll have a fire burning in the stove to lessen the chill in the shop while he patiently shapes the wood on the lathe.

Our annual ritual starts after fall's final harvest, hand in hand with the first frost. There is something soothing in the planning. George and I are blessed with many good friends. Our tradition of making friendship gifts helps us slow down and spend time thinking about the richness this adds to our lives.

When it comes time to making a decision about the gift, we consult our list. George and I discuss whether the ideas we've collected throughout the year have universal appeal. Will women use it as often as men? Do our "urban" friends have a need for it as much as our "farming" friends? We judge the options using Alfred Dunhill's maxim: "It must be useful. It must work dependably. It must be beautiful. It must last." Once we've settled on the idea, and determine how many we need to make, we construct a prototype.

This is where our personality differences come into full

play. George is an analyzer. I am more spontaneous. He wants to spend time on the prototype phase, perfecting the design. I want to start the production run right away!

Sitting at my sewing table, I show George the first sample napkin.

"Try the next one with white thread," he urges.

"The turquoise thread contrasts better," I say, knowing that he will have to see one made both ways before he will be satisfied.

In the early years of our marriage, our gifts emerged from the wood shop. We constructed rectangular boxes filled with paperwhite bulbs, Shaker peg clothes racks, and recipe card boxes shaped like miniature houses.

About five years ago, gift-making materials expanded to include fabric. We've made canvas carrying bags that our friends fill with food and gear and bring to our annual holiday gathering at a local ski lodge. The next winter, potholders printed with a seed package motif paraded out of my sewing room.

Another year, we made patchwork pillows rimmed in piping. I remember coming home from work during the last mad rush to finish our gifts. It was mid-December. My two sons, home on holiday break, were sitting on the couch, Nat stuffing polyester fiberfill into pillows I'd pieced before leaving for work that morning and Josh carefully hand-stitching the hole closed; the *Messiah* was providing inspiration in the background.

This past year we built birdhouses out of cedar posts from the dismantled fence on our farm. The fence, a victim of the February flood, provided poignant fodder for our holiday message: "*Made from old-growth Western Red Cedar that stood for 200 to 800 years in the Willamette Valley, the wood served as fence posts on our farm for the following 50 years. Salvaged out of the flood, it takes on a new form as home for our feathered friends.*"

One friend, Mary, sent us a card that read, "We just mounted [the birdhouse] in a tree which we can see from the kitchen window. We want to let you know how much we appreciate your workmanship and imagination year after year. You are in my thoughts every time I use one of your gifts. The violet green swallows are back again and looking for a house."

I anticipate the visit when we deliver our creations to family and friends. Giving the gift is a celebration itself, as it assures us that we will make time to see each friend during the holidays.

The repetitive motions of making friendship gifts calms my holiday-weary mind. I find that I'm concentrating, not on how many cookies I have left to bake or holiday cards I have yet to send, but rather on tender moments spent with friends. Moments that, over the years, have kept my life whole and unbroken. Relationships built piece by piece, shaped and lovingly sanded to smooth out any rough edges.

Church of Carson Hot Springs

Our search for spiritual renewal has led George and me to three different churches. The sermons at one no longer touch my soul. The second church was filled with those in search of a quick fix. Yet another church fails to fill my spiritual emptiness. Our annual return to Carson Hot Springs in southwest Washington substitutes as a pilgrimage of sorts; we seek an alternative place of worship.

We wake early and drive east to Carson Hotel and bathhouse, anticipating an experience I think of as ablution (a cleansing ritual). Our reservations are at 8:30 a.m., the first they schedule for Sunday morning—the same time as church service at home.

Carson Hotel, built in 1908, is tucked into a hollow along the Wind River. The river's namesake blows as we arrive. The mineral-laden water arrives via hydraulic pump from under the riverbed into the soaking tubs in the bathhouse. This water has put the hotel on the map.

The facade of the building lists to the left a bit, no doubt the result of an inadequate foundation. We park in the hotel lot and exit the car to see-your-breath cold outside with traces of rain dripping from the fir trees.

The lobby resembles a living room, with couches and chairs covered in faded chintz fabric. Crocheted throws conceal the threadbare upholstery. I sense a funky, yet monastic feel to the place. The room is filled with hushed expectancy.

The bathhouse divides down the middle. Warm, moist

air surrounds me as I enter the women's side, like a penitent seeking forgiveness. On the men's side, George gives himself over to the same ritual. We paid only eighty dollars for two baths, two body wraps and two massages, a bargain in 1990. An hour-long massage costs fifty dollars; thirty minutes of reflexology costs twenty dollars.

In the bathhouse, deliciously deep, claw-footed tubs line the walls, five feet apart. The tub's porcelain has mellowed to cream. The beadboard ceiling and walls, painted milky white, remind me of the kitchen in my grandmother's American Foursquare house in Delta, Colorado. White vinyl curtains hang loosely between the tubs on skinny iron bars. Stacks of white towels form a barrier of sorts where you stop and hand over your ticket.

No more than eight feet across, the changing room forces a shared intimacy among strangers in this different place of worship. I shed my heavy winter clothes and emerge naked, ready to fully enter into the sacrament of the moment. These waters substitute for the baptism I never had.

I realize how much I need this inspirational antidote. I want more of this spaciousness in my life so I can exercise slowness.

As I lay in the bath, the quiet penetrates, muffling the thoughts swirling in my busy mind. Bursts of chatter occasionally punctuate the still room as groups of women enter the bathhouse. Between the cracks in the curtain, I watch attendants—clad in white and flushed from the heat—fill each tub as those in need of purification arrive. The tub to my left begins to fill, while an attendant tells the woman to my right that her body wrap is ready. Her tub drains, the water escaping in a loud, gurgling suction of sound. The attendant brings me a sacrament of lemon-flavored water in a small paper cup. The ritual of communion.

After a twenty-minute soak, I pull my languid body from the deep tub and move in silence thirty feet to the wrap room along a narrow walkway of rubber mats laid end to end. Sixteen cots line both walls of the room. An attendant encases me in swaddling clothes: a cotton sheet, covered by a wool blanket. She places a towel over my eyes to block all light and distraction. I am left to sweat.

I enter a place of heightened awareness. The hymn of blood moving through my veins, air filling and escaping my lungs, suspends time. Each moment elongates into the next until I believe that I am a messenger of peace.

Twenty minutes later, my masseuse gently retrieves me from this dream world. I feel emptied and light. She guides me into a small room. I lay on the massage table. She spreads warm oil on my back and commences to resurrect my body. Her powerful hands cradle me through this transformation. This simple act, a benediction.

The ritual of cleansing, cocooning, and cradling imbues a blessed silence and spaciousness into my soul, fusing the deep divisions of mind, body, and heart.

Accelerate. Focus. Explode.

In the boathouse, the coxswain calls out, "Hands on, ready and lift, up to shoulders, walk it out." The deceptive weight of this svelte-looking shell forces us to sway until we can steady our knees and lock our elbows with the boat overhead. We walk the boat down to the dock. The coxswain bellows, "Roll to waist, ready and down." Miraculously the shell lands in the water right side up and none of us fall in.

We step gingerly into the tipping two-foot-wide shell. "Count down from bow when ready!" Her voice brings us back to the task at hand. We push off from the dock. We balance the sixty-foot-long shell on the still water as we make our way across Dexter Reservoir, twenty miles southeast of Eugene, Oregon.

It is our first row together as a team. Our goal: compete in the Frostbite Regatta at Green Lake in Seattle, Washington, in November. It is mid-July—only sixteen weeks to will our bodies into racing form.

I am assigned a starboard oar, bow position. At the coxswain's command, "Ready, row," we slide back, arms pulling blades through the water. For a moment we stroke together in a discordant rhythm, then we find our form and within a few strokes we are gliding across the water as one. It's a powerful feeling.

I'm hooked.

The team—Oregon Association of Rowers (OAR)—includes eight women and our male coach. Rowers' average

age: forty-two.

Six weeks later we push off from the dock as the sun breaks over the hills to the east. The bow four still struggle, though the stern four look pretty good. We practice "catch drills," so our oars will all enter the water at the same time, making our stroke more efficient. Slowly we learn the intricate dance involved in becoming a team.

We row the distance of our race—a thousand meters— four times. The only sound is the creak of the riggers and the plop of the blades as they enter the water. Coach Craig hovers alongside in the motorboat, barking commands. "Catch together. Fast hands away. Use your legs. Put some power into it." Our fastest time is 4:20—far longer than our 3:52 goal. Hugely satisfying, nonetheless.

It's the first time in my life I admit out loud that I am competitive. I have spent so long throttling my ambition; now I want my team to see the whole me. Rowing makes me feel more alive. While scrubbing myself in the shower, I notice biceps that could win at arm wrestling and hamstrings that are boxy and hard. I have muscles.

Nine weeks to race day— we have a wonderful row this evening over silky smooth water under a full moon. It's almost Zen-like. Just two days later, however, a litany of admonitions runs through my head during the entire workout: Reach farther forward on your catch. Faster hands at the finish.

The act of rowing takes intense, whole-body concentration. Drive backward with thigh and calf muscles. Squeeze the oar into the stomach. Once in the finish position, bend forward from the waist before bringing the knees up into a forward slide. Catch, drive, finish, slide. Focus.

We seek perfect synchronization, blades moving in continuous, fluid motion. When all eight oars catch together, all you can hear is *cha*—the sound of mastery. Rowing is the ultimate team sport. Eight women step into the boat as one body. Catch together. Hands away together. Swing in unison. Slide together.

I have never been athletic. At twenty-one I played my

sport—racquetball. Now, at forty-one, I'm on a team of rowers; we've hired a coach and will compete in a sanctioned race in another state. How did this happen?

Three weeks to race day—we practice race starts. Brief, breathless strokes get the boat moving from a standstill to thirty strokes per minute within the first fifty feet of the race. The coxswain chants like an auctioneer, "Sit ready. Ready. Row."

Then we practice power tens. We push back so hard with our thigh and calf muscles that we rise up out of our seats. Now I understand why our shoes are bolted into the boat.

At home I make subtle adjustments in my lifestyle to ensure that I will be whole on race day. The night before workouts I go to bed early. I wake up at 6:30 a.m. to stretch, eat something, digest, then drive to the lake. Where is the person who used to sleep in on weekends?

One week to race day—our last practice. At Dexter, the water moves in half-foot-high rollers, coming up through the dock like something alive. The fall wind ices in toward shore. Everything is glassy, brilliant, and fresh. Our coxswain manages to push us to a 4:06 time.

November 13, 1999. Race day. It is overcast and misting heavily, but the water is smooth. A perfect day for racing. Coach gives our pre-race pep talk. "This is it. You can do this. You're athletes."

The race official confirms the starting lineup. "Lake Union, Kenai, University of Oregon, Alaska, OAR." My stomach ties itself in a knot. The race aligner calls out, "OAR hold your position." Our coxswain says, "Sit ready."

The race official bellows, "Attention. Go!" And just like that, the race begins.

Our start is incredible. The cox yells, "Your rate is thirty-six!" Faster than we have ever started. We move out in front of the other four boats. "Power ten," she commands. We stay even with the UO team in lane three. We surge past the Kenai crew.

"Accelerate! ... Focus! ... Explode!" I can't tell where we

are. Have we passed the eight-hundred-meter buoy? Are we in the final sprint? Cheers from the dock grow louder. The horn goes off. We cross the finish line. Two boats have yet to cross. We've come in third. Ten seconds behind the UO boat—rowers' average age: twenty.

We are athletes!

Reluctant Spirit in Training

Driving through rush-hour traffic like the frenetic, habitually late person that I am, I try to get to the Siddha Yoga Meditation Center before class starts.

Once class gets underway with everyone meditating, it's difficult to sneak in unnoticed. Even from her likeness framed on the wall, Guramaya notices. She gazes at me from the front of the room with heavy-lidded, all-knowing eyes.

Because we have never been formally introduced, I am, understandably, a bit shaky on the pronunciation of her name. During dinner with my husband after our fifth yoga class, I finally get a clue about her name because of the funny look George gives me when I make a remark about how Guramaya's eyes follow you during meditation—like those holographs in the Haunted Mansion at Disneyland.

He says, simply, "It's Guru Mayi."

"Ohhh." The light dawns. She's a guru.

Where was I? Being late. The class members notice we are late, but, they are too acutely polite to mention the fact that it's usually George or me delaying their transcendence into the stillness of the mind.

This month we focus on the auspicious state of the mind. In order to reflect on this, we contort our desk-bound bodies into different asanas, or postures. In the yogic view, the body is a temple of spirit, the care of which is an important stage in one's spiritual growth. The practice of asana is supposed to help you develop the habit of discipline and the ability to concentrate, both of which are necessary for meditation.

The postures fall into the following categories: standing, seated, supine (lying on the back), prone (lying face down), and inversions. Inversions sounds like a word my body won't do. Asana practice is supposed to create flexibility to get into the position, build strength to hold the pose in proper alignment, and develop stamina to maintain it for longer durations.

Class one: on our tiny yoga pads, we attempt Salabha, the locust.

"Lie on the floor, face down, with your feet together, toes stretching back, arms at your side. Straighten your knees." This feels good.

"Turn your palms up. Raise your arms parallel to the floor and stretch them back. Press your pubic bone into the floor, tilt your pelvis to protect your lower back. Inhale and raise your head and chest off the floor." One class member, The Graceful One, moves smoothly, as fluid as silk.

I look up. In the silent room, my classmates have transformed into a flock of swans, ready for takeoff; a formation of B-15s, with tight buttock muscles, prepared to taxi the runway; a school of barracudas floating in the Sea of Cortez. The incongruous images float in my mind. I always seem to be the doer and the observer at the same time. Maybe it is my protection against getting too deeply enmeshed in just one thing.

Time for the next asana.

"Standing postures help build strength and stability, getting us grounded and centered. Vrksasana, the tree pose, *gives* a beautiful upward stretch and a sense of balance." As our teacher demonstrates the pose, it appears to me that it *takes* a sense of balance. But I'm game.

"Stand in Tadasana, the mountain pose."

"Ground into the floor through the balls of both feet. Extend upward through your stomach." This I can do.

"Place your hands on your hips. Now, move your center of balance onto your left foot. Bend your right leg out to the side, hold your foot with your right hand and bring the sole of your right foot into the top of your left inner thigh." I try to be present in the moment, without obsessing on what's next on the to-do list. I think about picking up groceries on the way home.

I bring the sole of my right foot up to my thigh, but it only wants to stay there for a brief rest before touching ground again. I catch myself from losing my balance by tapping my right foot on the ground and bringing it back up to my thigh. I repeat this four times in quick succession, feeling like I should have on toe shoes and a tutu.

Meanwhile, George takes the hard-line approach. He teeters precariously on his left leg, looking seasick, employing elaborate means to achieve the balance of a tree, unwilling to move that right foot until it comes thudding down onto the floor in a very unmeditative kind of way. We try again, this time with the arms.

"Extend your arms to the sides, turn the palms up, then stretch your arms over your head. Join the palms, keeping the elbows straight. Breathe evenly and balance."

I find a moment of balance this time. George, however, thuds into the door behind him. I burst out laughing.

Yoga class makes me feel like a little girl again—trying so hard to have good manners at the dinner table when company came, that I would end up in hysterics from holding it all in. There are no class rules, but I seem to have already committed several faux pas. It's like not talking in church. There are no clues to signal correct behavior, except for the noticeable whisper that everyone uses to greet each other. Class members have been most accommodating, though. Once I start chortling at my inability to twist my body into a difficult pose, they laugh along with me, quietly at first, as though having been given permission.

Just last night, the Cow Face position proved particularly vexing. With arms (supposedly) clasped behind my back as though I am attempting to scratch a place I can't quite reach, and my legs scissored under me with my rump balanced precariously on my thighs, someone had the audacity to ask, "Just why is this called the Cow Face pose?" I let out a low moo. The classmate with the Sanskrit name I can't pronounce answers with a definitive snort. The Graceful One joins the barnyard noises with a surprisingly realistic mmmoooooo. My body is more like a barn than a temple.

How did two meat-eating, gin-drinking Type A's find themselves barefoot and cross-legged on Monday nights, chanting Sanskrit? George ran into his cousin Jessie who has been teaching yoga for twelve years. They got to talking about George's sciatica. Jessie encouraged George to come to her next class. The rest is history.

I am not one to read instructions before tackling something new. I am what they call a kinesthetic learner. After six classes, I decide it's time to read a bit about this "exercise program" I have innocently taken up. It turns out Siddha Yoga is an ancient spiritual tradition passed on through a lineage of self-realized masters known as siddhas, or perfected ones. Now there's something to shoot for. Swami Chidvilasananda, also known as Gurumayi, is the Living Master of this lineage. Hence, her picture hanging in the place of honor, over the empty chair with empty wooden thongs where her feet would be if she were sitting in the chair.

After last class, I complimented The Graceful One on, you guessed it, her gracefulness. She seemed truly surprised and shimmered in pleasure.

"How long have you been taking yoga?" I ask, trying to get a sense of the challenge ahead.

"Since I was fifteen," she answers with a quiet incredulity, like she can't quite believe it has been that long.

Now, here is a woman who is a good ten years older than me, which means she has been contorting her body for thirty years. *Thirty years*. I read further in the book. There are, it seems, hundreds of asanas to master, all with incredibly long names.

George's sciatica has improved, so we decide to skip the

next eight-week series. I do hope to get back to it at some point. As with many things, I like the *idea* of yoga but can't seem to find time in my schedule to *practice*.

So far, my favorite pose is Savasana, the corpse pose. Once the posture is mastered, quietness can be called upon at will. Then my body will be a temple of spirit.

Searching for My Father

With only a photo of my grandfather, Vasillios Konstantine "Pappy" Papaspyridis; the name of the village where he grew up, Kandyla; and a picture of a man named Kostas, who we think is my grandfather's cousin—I set off for Greece with my husband. I have yearned for years to make this journey to trace my father's roots, to fill the hole he left inside when he died.

At Heathrow Airport, I glance surreptitiously at the men waiting to board Olympic Air Flight 260 from London to Athens. In each face I see, I am looking for my father—that familiar high forehead, creased in perpetual surprise at life, a rounded nose, and thick black eyebrows that almost meet in the middle.

In a time before Ancestry.com exists, I know but few facts: that my grandfather emigrated from Greece through Ellis Island in 1906 at the age of seventeen, settled in Colorado Springs, adopted the language and customs of America—and never looked back. Growing up in Southern California, few stories of Poppy's homeland ever reached me. A search through family records unearthed only my grandfather's citizenship certificate and a few photos. I began to think of myself as an emissary to a distant time.

I hope to find answers to some questions about my father and myself: why this last name, Pappas, is so important to me; why I can't seem to communicate without waving my hands for emphasis; and why my pride gets in the way of making amends.

As our taxi driver accelerates toward Piraeus, the hot

Mediterranean night blasts through the window. I am in my element: this dry heat is in my blood. I ask our driver about searching for family, and I immediately feel at home when he responds to my questions by taking both hands off the wheel to talk.

Every Greek I visit with delivers an opinion on how I should try to find my relatives. One store owner says, in that direct, declarative way of speaking that reminds me of my father: "You go to Red Cross first, then you go to president of community, and then police." For emphasis he repeats the sequence, then nods, agreeing with himself.

Anna, our friend who is serving as translator, meets us at her sister-in-law, Xeni's, house. Anna brings out the Athens phone book and together we look up the name Papaspyridis. We place a call to K. Papaspyridis, the most likely prospect among the fifteen names listed.

A man answers the phone. He confirms—in Greek, and then in English—that he is Kostas, and that his uncle was Vasillios, my grandfather. Anna hands me the phone. There is so much I want to say, but choked with emotions, I mostly listen. Kostas' welcoming voice pulses through the phone, heavily enriched with drawn-out consonants. My heart beats hard as he recalls meeting my two uncles, Denny and Gordon, in Colorado Springs in 1958. He invites us to come the next morning to his house.

Kostas greets us at the gate to his home in Athens. I recognize him from the forty-year-old picture tucked in my plastic baggie! We gather on a couch in the living room. I turn on my tape recorder, not wanting to miss one moment. Kostas, seventy, is a chain smoker just like my dad. Unlike my dad, he is a talker and I can't get enough. As ash builds up on cigarette after cigarette, stories—lost to me until now—unfold.

Kostas grew up in a large family, with eight brothers and sisters. Kostas' father, Alexandros, is one of my grandfather's four siblings. Their father, Kostis—my great-grandfather—operated a general store at the family house that he built in Kandyla in 1886.

When Kostas learns that we plan to be in Kandyla the following day, which happens to be election day, he calls his brother Athanassios to tell him about our visit. Many of Kostas' brothers and sisters—my great-uncles and great-aunts—will be staying at the family house, their traditional voting address. Kostas explains, "Once you get to the village, ask anyone where the Papaspyridis house is. They will know."

On Sunday morning, we travel west to Tripoli, then north through farms filled with grapevines and wheat, into hills that become mountains. Kandyla is nestled at the inverted apex of three steep, dry mountains. We arrive to find the village square overflowing with men in gray and black, sitting at tables and talking in groups in the street. I anxiously study this unfamiliar scene. The momentum that has propelled me forward from Oregon to Athens and now to Kandyla comes to a standstill along with the car. I clutch my plastic baggie full of pictures of my grandfather and the family tree I have tried unsuccessfully to reconstruct. Having focused so much on the "search" itself, I feel unprepared for the actual meeting.

Like a child on the first day of kindergarten, I approach the Papaspyridis house with a mixture of excitement and fear. The large, two-story stone house with green shutters looks closed, but the garden gate hangs open. I poke my head around the gate and see a teenager sitting on a chair, as though she has been waiting for me. And, indeed, she has. She yelps, "Hello," jumps up and runs through the kitchen door shouting, "She's here!"

Relatives pour out the door and surround me with a warmth that spreads through my skin, opening my pores. I meet Ioanna and Eleni, Anathassios and Georgios, Anastasia and Thalia, Chyrsoula and Ionnis. I frantically try to keep everyone straight. I don't want to embarrass all the Pappas family I represent. They welcome me so warmly that my nervousness quickly subsides.

There is so much kissing and hugging compared to my family of reluctant emoters. I feel enthralled to be in a room where such effusiveness is commonplace. We beam at each other, exchange family information, and all talk at once with *lots* of hand gesturing. I recognize the raised-eyebrows and high forehead so familiar from my father's face. I discover that many of my second cousins are engineers, just like my dad. I try to write everything down, to get conversations on tape—but finally abandon the efforts, to luxuriate in the moment. The warmth of these father-figures makes my blood sing through my veins and my heart expands to encompass my "new" family.

Anastasia and Georgios pull out a family photo album. Together, we thumb through the yellowed pages. I see pictures of my uncles Denny and Gordon. Vasillios must have sent these back home to Kandyla. He stayed connected after all. And then I spot a picture of my mom and dad on their wedding day! One more piece of evidence that I am home, anchored to this place, these people. I close my eyes to keep my heart from bursting. In one of the kindest gestures, Georgios pulls the picture out of the photo album and hands it to me.

Ioanna stays busy in the kitchen preparing sausages and roasting pork and potatoes. Eleni leads George through the garden. A snapdragon grows wedged between two steps on the stairway. It blooms each year in the same place, ever since Eleni can remember. She collects its seeds and hands them to us to plant in our garden—a reminder of everyone and everything that has gone before.

We sit down to eat surrounded by smiles and serving platters piled with potatoes, meat, and cheese. We toast the good fortune that brings us together in this special place. Anathassios fills my plate; Georgios fills my wine glass. Neither go empty for the next two hours. My relatives admonish me, "Eat more. Eat more!" It is impossible to say no. After the meal, we visit the cemetery where my great-grandmother, Theodora, is buried. We walk among blindingly white marble crosses and headstones to reach her grave. Cool green cypress trees, pointing toward heaven, surround the parched grounds. Standing at her grave a circle closes, enfolding me in grace.

We leave my relatives in Kandyla with promises to call them in Athens before we return to Oregon.

After a rushed five-day tour of the Peloponnese, we head north toward Athens and our final evening in Greece.

Once again, George and I sit at a table surrounded by great-aunts and great-uncles. The room fills with laughter when these brothers and sisters come together. We discuss the recent election in Kandyla. I tell them about my strong conviction to participate in making my community a better place. That I always vote Democrat. That my dad always voted Democrat. I receive effusive claps of approval on my shoulder. Kostas says, "Of course. It is because Kandyla has a long democratic tradition." This simple statement makes the strong connection I've always felt with my father's politics infinitely clear and right.

Finding these long-lost relations—whose lives contain so much joy—adds richness to my life. They expand my sense of family.

No Time to Die

After my mom has spent seven days in the hospital, we hear the words that everyone dreads. "There's nothing more we can do for your mother."

Mom, at eighty-four, has accumulated a litany of woes—diabetes, Parkinson's, and liver disease, plus no short-term memory due to dementia associated with Parkinson's. Her body can no longer heal.

After one more night in the hospital, Mom will be released to hospice care. My sister, my husband, and I meet with the social worker and the nurse. Should we move her to a nursing home with twenty-four-hour care, with a doctor that visits and a nurse always on the premises? Or return Mom to the assisted living facility where she's lived for more than two years—to a familiar place where the caregivers know and love her? This would require arranging for round-the-clock nursing coverage through an in-home nursing agency.

The social worker explains the advantages and disadvantages of each path. Sallie and I struggle with the decision. I feel helpless with these huge questions, not wanting to do anything to hasten Mom's demise. Then we have the brilliant idea of asking Mom. She votes for returning to her room at the assisted living facility.

As I wheel her down the hospital corridor to leave the next morning, Mom, who has not opened her eyes for several days, looks alert and almost giddy at the idea of leaving the hospital. I point out the blooming jonquils. She jokes with the Handi-Cab driver.

<u>Hospice. Day 1.</u> Mom sits in her recliner, bright-eyed and in good spirits. Did we do the right thing, committing to hospice when she looks better than she did before she went to the emergency room? Hospice is for those who have less than six months to live. Maybe the doctor was wrong.

The social worker assigned to our family reassures me that this is the "hospice effect." When people get their meds corrected, get released from the antiseptic environment of the hospital, and have loved ones around, they often physically and mentally rebound for a short time.

Meantime, my career has shifted into overdrive. As Interim City Manager, I am trying to keep the wheels on the truck until the newly hired City Manager arrives in town. We are in the middle of negotiating four union contracts, trying to fund operations at a proposed new jail, working to fill numerous vacancies in our Public Works Department, and drafting an update to our Emergency Management Plan. And the budget is due—all the normal things that keep a city running.

I am living inside out. Crying at unexpected moments, confused and raw. Trying to get my mind around the idea of easing Mom's pain rather than fighting for her life.

<u>Day 3.</u> Mom received morphine twice during the night for pain and looks exhausted and loopy when I stop in to see her the next day.

She is bewildered by the number of new faces near her, tending to her, asking questions. As am I. Is it Tammy on day shift and Sarah on swing shift? And how do I trust these women I've never met to care about my mom? Will they treat her kindly? Will they wipe her brow with a hot washcloth—one of her favorite relaxation techniques? Will they meld their ways with the caregivers at the assisted living facility, or will there be personality conflicts? I have no energy for any pettiness, any neediness on the part of anyone, except for my mom.

<u>Day 4.</u> "Who are all these people?" my sweet mother asks. I explain to her that she is very sick and they are

taking care of her. We repeat this conversation many times over the next few weeks.

Day 7. "We're just playing a waiting game now, right?" Mom asks me abruptly, knocking the wind out of me. Until now, she has been the Queen of Denial. This is a new, honest twist.

"That's not how I look at it, Mom. I feel lucky for every day I get to see you." There is a long silence while she absorbs the words.

"I do too," she says, finally.

Day 8. "So, Mom, what's on your mind today?"

Mom responds, "Who says I have a mind? I think I left it somewhere a couple of weeks ago."

She seems chatty, so I continue. "Do you think I should write a book about witty sayings of my mom?"

"It would be a short book!"

I want to bottle these precious moments so I can take them out later, turn them over in my hands, and marvel at this special woman: my mother who has given me unconditional love my entire life.

Today a call from the city's Human Resources Manager interrupts my visit with Mom. She needs authority to make a final financial offer to the firefighters' union to avoid arbitration. Life seems too short for costly arbitration, which can create ill will. I give direction to spend the money and settle.

That afternoon, my prince of a husband, George, stops in for a visit with us. Mom expresses confusion about why she can't "get a ticket out of here."

Trying to instill comfort, George says, "Don't worry, Pat, you're going to a better place."

She rolls her eyes, "I don't know about that."

I smile to myself. She will not let go of this world easily.

I receive another phone call. One of our police officers failed to appropriately "clear" the intersection and hit a vehicle on his way to a call, injuring the driver. Adrenalin surges through my veins. Two hours later, my staff calls back to let me know the driver has been treated and released from the hospital. I have trouble being present in two worlds: work and Mom's.

Day 9. A mallard pair has appeared in the courtyard outside Mom's window, delighting her. She remembers them from last year! My sister and I, along with the help of a nursing assistant, help her stand so she can get a full look at them as they feed on the sunflower seeds that have fallen below her bird feeder. The effort leaves Mom exhausted.

Day 10. Mom seems very tired this afternoon when Sallie and I visit with her. We look at old photos together. I hand Mom a photo of Aunt Billie and Uncle Bill, my dad's sister and brother-in-law. Mom asks, "They're all gone now?"

Sallie tells her they have all passed on.

"You two are all that's left?"

Sallie responds, "No, Mom. There are cousins: Pennie and Gerrie, David and Linda, Pam, and Jan and Bob."

Mom says, "You two will have to carry on."

After I get home that evening, I realize that Mom was passing the torch on to the next generation—us. This flashing back and forth between being present with her line of thinking and then, later, realizing what the conversation means, gives me emotional whiplash. I feel drained.

Day 11. "Are they going to get him an office?" It takes me a minute to track what she's saying.

"You mean George?"

"Well, he's here so much. ..." Her question makes sense when I realize that George, as the lead organizer for an upcoming Democratic party gala, has received numerous frantic phone calls while visiting Mom. Putting two and two together, the office space question seems logical.

George has been a stalwart in these last days and weeks of Mom's decline. He can get her to talk about things that she might not ever mention to me. And he makes her laugh. He has the freedom of not being *of* her, but loving her, nonetheless.

That evening, George relays to me a great story about the club Mom says she helped found at her high school:

WIW. I'm thinking it has something to do with the war? But no, the war had not even started yet during her high school years. Laughing, George says, "It stands for Wild Independent Women!" That's my mom!

On one visit, George reassures Mom. "Pat, you've done such a wonderful job raising beautiful daughters. I'm so grateful for Cindy."

One of those long Pappas pauses. "Well, I'm not dead yet."

"I know!" George says, "but I wanted to tell you that anyway."

She's such a tough cookie. Doesn't let in a lot of emotion. I have always been the one in my family to express my feelings. Every visit, every conversation I have about my mom leaves me feeling like a seeping wound.

"Take the time you need," say my co-workers and the elected officials I work for. How do I possibly translate that? The time I need is the next twenty years. I will be orphaned when my mom goes. My family history diminishes that much more. Who will be the glue to hold my sister and me together? We know a few family stories, but they are only abbreviated versions of the whole.

<u>Day 15.</u> The hospice nurse says she sees a "noticeable decline in function." I head home and email cousins and long-distance friends about Mom's condition ... suddenly my computer screen flashes: "Windows is shutting down." So, I realize, is Mom.

I envisioned hospice to be peaceful: candles burning, the lights dimmed with my mom lying in bed with her eyes closed. Not this adrenalin switch going off and on with the ups and downs of a roller coaster ride. The good days are so good and the bad days are so bad. There is no in-between. When am I supposed to have the conversation about where her spirit will go and give us both some sense of closure? Anytime I get too close to asking about her feelings, she quickly veers away. As though driving the car, she makes sharp right-hand turns when sensing trouble ahead. Driving and showing her emotions were never her strong suit.

Day 18. I tell Mom I'm going home to watch the Academy Awards. We long ago bonded over clothing design with all of her sewing projects during my childhood. I ask what she thinks the stars' dresses will look like this year. She says, "More tailored." She is a fashion maven to the end.

Days later, I buy a *People* magazine so I can show her pictures of the dresses from the Oscars. As we thumb through the pages together, she looks at one dress and says, "No one should wear a dress that color." It's canary yellow. I agree.

We Pappases don't do short goodbyes. We say goodbye and then think of one more thing we forgot to share or one more distraction to lengthen the leave-taking. Is this a form of politeness or some strange family aberration? George teases me about it mercilessly. Now it gets harder and harder for Mom to let Sallie or me leave, as though she might not be there when we return. She asks for one more favor. Or brings up something she's already mentioned earlier in the visit.

Day 22. Mom barely opens her eyes and refuses food. Every day when I visit, I smooth her wiry gray hair back from her forehead and hold my hand on the crown of her head. Today, when I am ready to leave and feeling too overwhelmed to talk, I kneel beside her and lean my head against her chest. She smooths my hair back from my forehead and holds her hand on the crown of my head.

Day 24. Mom moves deeper and deeper into another world. Most of the time she is in her room. But then she fixes her gaze upward, focusing on a corner of the room where the ceiling meets the wall, and disappears. Eyes closed, unable to answer questions. Checking out.

My mother's love of teddy bears is apparent. Teddy bears perch everywhere in her room. One of the nursing assistants brings in a bear with wildly unkempt fur dressed in a chenille vest. She tells my mom she found the bear running down the hall trying to find her room. Her generous gesture brings a wry smile to Mom's face, and the new bear joins the collection, evidence that the caregivers we have hired to provide twenty-four-hour care have taken to her.

Today my husband tells me that I need to check back in on life, that I am not leaving with my mom. Part of me feels that she and I are traveling on opposing parallel tracks of some sort. I sleep less and less while Mom sleeps fourteen to sixteen hours a day. I wake up at three every morning. As Mom eats less and less, I stuff myself with food. Food has always been a source of comfort. If you're worried, eat. If you're happy, eat! If you're sad, eat some more. It's my Greek heritage. And that is exactly what I do, filling the space that Mom no longer inhabits.

I experience extreme difficulty concentrating. I can't seem to get through a paragraph of a work memo without having to reread it for meaning. Emails from work pile up. I attempt to craft an optimistic memo describing the proposed budget. But my hope and optimism are all used up right now. Work decisions remain background noise to the more important unfolding in my life.

<u>Day 33.</u> Mom sleeps deeply, snoring and sweating profusely. Her nightgown and bedding need changing every two hours. Her blood sugar is dangerously low. Is she unconscious or on her journey down the pathway? She has slept for twenty-seven hours at this point, and has had nothing to eat or drink. Sallie and I struggle with what to do next, but at eleven that night, Mom wakes up and says, "I'm hungry." Astounding. The roller coaster builds back up to a bigger high, which means a lower low comes next.

I've been dreaming about driving down Topanga Canyon to Zuma Beach on a hot summer's day. Sallie tells me she's been having similar dreams about happy places in our childhood. I sort back through the years. Riding in the green Ford station wagon to pick up Dad from work. Tent camping at Lone Pine. Driving through the Mojave Desert at two in the morning in a thunderstorm with lightning streaking through the air. Eating fish sticks for Friday night dinner. Finding hidden Easter "nests" full of jelly beans on our indoor Easter egg hunts. My mom pedaling me to kindergarten at Enadia Way Elementary School on the back of her faded purple three-speed Schwinn. Weekends camping at Lake Cachuma and the bass tournaments my dad competed in. Girl Scout meetings at Shadow Ranch Park. Disneyland. Air raid drills. Mom sewing Barbie doll clothes. Picking plums and peaches in the backyard. The 1968 Ford Mustang. Fourth of July pool parties in the backyard. Watching the fireworks at Lanark Park. Fabric stores. Sewing. *Mutual of Omaha's Wild Kingdom. The Ed Sullivan Show.*

I can only imagine Mom's list. Dancing to big bands at Manitou Springs, Colorado. Watching the Model Ts make it up the Pike's Peak Hill Climb. Waitressing at the Gold Nugget, owned by my grandfather. Canning apricots and peaches in the kitchen. Growing ranunculus, gladiolas, calla lilies, and trumpet vine in the hot Southern California summers. Fishing at Lake Casitas. Troop leader of Girl Scout Troop 2089. Spending time with her best friend Jackie, laughing together. Camping at Twin Lakes and Lake Mary. Sewing ... always sewing.

As Easter approaches, I think about the dresses my mom made for Sallie and me each spring. We loved the identical dresses of light blue, full-skirted cotton with crinolines to make them twirl better! So many beautiful dresses. I wish I had kept them all.

Day 37. I feel anchorless. Mom's space-time continuum has fallen apart. She doesn't understand how the caregivers suddenly appear in her room (when I've pushed the call button for assistance). Nor where they've gone when they leave. She keeps saying, "Amazing." I agree with her that life is amazing and I'm so happy to share it with her.

She says a large bird came to the birdbath outside her window. And then somehow the bird stood on her shelf over the refrigerator in her room. Is she thinking about flying away?

Day 38. Mom tells me in an incredulous voice, "I woke up this morning and I was here. I couldn't believe it."

Something keeps pulling her back from her journey.

"Where did you think you'd be?" I ask. Silence. She has gone traveling again.

Day 40. The hospice nurse has given an order to cease all medication since my mom can no longer swallow. She has had no food or liquid for almost forty-eight hours. I keep telling her that she doesn't have to be so strong anymore, that it's okay to let go. She can't talk, but she does acknowledge my presence and tries to form the words to respond. Always, when I leave at the end of a visit, I say, "I love you, Mom." And she answers, "I love you too." This evening when I say, "I love you," Mom says "unnhh."

"Mom, are you trying to say I love you, too?"

"Ummmm."

"I know you do." Driving home, I feel wiped out and disoriented.

Day 41. I bring Lucy, my German shorthair in to visit Mom one last time: grandma visiting grandma. Lucy will be fourteen years old next month. Her hips are bad and her time is limited. I place a dog bone in my mom's hand and hold it there because Mom can no longer hold onto anything. Lucy comes up to the side of the bed and gently takes it from her.

Day 44. Easter. Tears sheet down my cheeks as I sit next to Mom's bed. I tell her about the birds eating at her feeder and bathing in the birdbath. She has been in a state of semi-consciousness for almost a week, but she can still hear me. Hearing is one of the last senses to go. We play a Frank Sinatra CD, her favorite. Her body is shutting down. I receive a call Easter morning from my lifelong friend in Yuma who is very in touch with the spiritual world. She believes today will be Mom's last. I agree. The final five days have been one last, long Pappas goodbye. Mom has been holding out for Easter.

She makes it to 7:52 a.m. on the day following Easter and then gently, peacefully, slips from our world into the next.

I love you, Mom. Be in peace.

Hair Dating

hair dating: *(n) the determination of the year of an old photograph by means of hairstyle*

Prior to flying down to Bodega Bay in Northern California for our twenty-second annual reunion, emails buzzed between the six of us: Eileen (FBI agent), Barb (with a passion for musicals), Mary (prom queen), Michele (DIY home improvement expert), Teri (oldest sister in a large Catholic family), and me. As the day of our get-together approached, the number of emails ratcheted up several notches, but we still couldn't agree on just how to mark our collective fortieth birthdays.

Should we, as Barb suggested, go skinny-dipping in the Pacific at midnight? It might be too cold. And what if we couldn't stay awake that late? Should we all get tattooed with a similar something to mark this significant milestone in our lives and in our friendship? What about dying and spiking our hair? No ... we'd be accused of trying to look young. As if we could!

My friends and I are the keepers of each other's past. Our journey together over the past twenty-two years has created a collective memory. We have shared each other's transformative moments: too many boyfriend break-ups to count, college graduations, marriages, new homes, births, miscarriages, celebrating career successes, mourning a sister's death, and the death of many of our parents.

Now geographically dispersed, we get together once

a year. The only rule for our annual gathering is no husbands and no kids—unless you're nursing.

Mary called. She was having trouble with *the rule*. Although daughter Grace, at three, was beyond nursing age, Mary agonized over whether to leave her behind for the weekend. Separation anxiety. The five of us decided that husband Peter could manage just fine. After many phone calls Mary finally acquiesced at the eleventh hour and left little Grace at home.

I had the idea of presenting each of my dear friends with a photo album to commemorate our fortieth birthday year. The album would contain pictures of the six of us at our various get-togethers since we graduated from high school in 1976. I searched through my photos for those prime shots, made color copies, and began to construct a running dialogue to accompany the photos.

But I had trouble placing events in time. I couldn't remember which year we attempted to hike in the Santa Barbara backcountry and got ordered out by rangers because of fire danger. Was it 1981? It couldn't have been because that's the year Barb got married and we skipped our normal get-together so we could all be in her wedding. So I included the pictures and left a blank spot for narrative.

What about the year my hair was in a wild perm? (Please don't let me do that again!) Was it in 1977, my freshman year at the University of California at Santa Barbara? Or was it the same year that Teri started med school? Who can remember? I left another blank spot for narrative and moved on. Finally, as the blank spots became more frequent, I decided to take one album with me and we'd reconstruct our past when we got together at the beach house.

Barb and Mary flew up from Southern California, Michele drove over from northeast California, and Eileen flew in from Chicago and landed at the same time as my flight from Oregon. Teri met us all at the airport and we made our way to Bodega Bay. Immediately, we got down to some serious chatting. The six of us have an extremely high chat quotient. I have to start practicing weeks before I see these dear friends of mine or, by mid-weekend, my jaw begins to ache. In the first five hours of our weekend, after covering our relationships with our mothers and the stages of growth of our children, and talking ourselves into intoxication, we dove back into the how-to-mark-our-fortieth dilemma.

Finally at 1 a.m., as we became more horizontal and less coherent, Michele suggested we get a third hole pierced in our ears. There were sleepy nods all around.

We drove into town the next day and giggled our way into the jewelry store. First, we had to decide if we should get a gold post or a cubic zirconium stud. We debated plain or fancy. It was unanimous: a cubic zirconium stud. We split three pairs of earrings and proceeded. Eileen went first. Based on the concern in Michele's eye, we decided she'd better go second before she could change her mind. Then Mary, Barb, and Teri went—and I was last. We looked so chic! The store owner snapped a photo with all of us pointing to our studs.

On the drive back to the beach house, we got a lot of mileage out of stud references and terminology. Studding around. Sleeping with your stud. Like thirteen-year-old schoolgirls, we were completely delighted with ourselves. We went out to dinner that night and flirted shamelessly with our waiter. Then we made bets on how long it would take our husbands and children to notice our new studs.

The odds favored my friends who have daughters in the ten- to thirteen-year-old range. They notice *everything* about how their mothers dress and are embarrassed by ninety-eight percent of it. "Oh Muther ... you can't wear that!"

Finally I brought out the photo album I had put together. As we age, faulty memory plagues all of us. Usually, when we combine all our brain power, we can land on the truth of an issue. Each of us helps construct a piece of the past.

As my friends leafed through the album, someone coined the term "hair dating" (as opposed to carbon dating) because that's what it really came down to: we determined the correct year and location of the photo by looking at our respective hairstyles over the years. And we laughed and laughed with that deep belly laugh that explodes from your gut when you are with those who can finish your sentences and finish your stories because they've heard them all before.

Since that long-ago gathering, we've been lucky enough to experience eighteen more annual reunions. I am grateful for this forty-year friendship. My relationship with these inspiring, strong women sustains me and best of all makes me laugh. Little Gracie just graduated from college and bears no permanent damage from her mom's weekend away with the girls. As for hair dating, at age fifty-seven we are all growing our hair long again. May we live to regret this!

Schooled by the Herd

Golden summer light slants through the cottonwoods at 6:30 a.m. as George and I move irrigation pipe across our pasture. It is forty-seven degrees. Our watering dance is down to a science. With each of us holding an end, in forty-five minutes we can move three lines of ten forty-foot pipes. At 6 p.m. we repeat the dance, only now it's eighty-seven degrees and sweat coats us like a second skin. It takes us four days to water the whole pasture. Ten days later we begin the dance all over again.

Once each lateral is complete, I let the water slowly back in from the main line. The cows act as if it's a game—they love to drink from the sprinkler heads as the water first starts to trickle out. With all three lines set and the pump operating at full pressure, the sprinklers shift into a satisfying *shick-shick-shick*.

Morning pipe moving becomes a birding meditation. A belted kingfisher *chidders* as it flies along Cedar Creek. A red-tailed hawk *screes* while lifting off from a massive cottonwood. Tree swallows sweep through the warming air, chasing midges. A great blue heron flaps away in dramatic departure.

We move pipe to keep the pasture green so we can feed our Black Angus and Murray Grey cows during this desicating summer. This year, our small herd of seven mamas, eight calves, eight yearlings, and a two-year-old keeps us plenty busy.

I grew up in suburban Los Angeles in a small stucco house with a yard that was just large enough to play wagon train or fetch with our beagle. I married a fifth-generation farmer who grew up on a hundred-acre dairy farm. He refers to his farming background as a congenital disorder.

We got into raising beef six years ago. George wanted to do something with our land besides growing hay. "We may as well get some cows and *use* the hay," he said. I had a demanding full-time-plus job and didn't pay much attention to the books by George's side of the bed: *New Zealand Fencing* and *How to Build a Corral*.

Before I knew it, George hired a young guy to help him build pasture fencing and the corral. Then it was time to populate our herd. When George said he wanted to raise cows, I was thinking maybe two or three—something interesting to look at out the living room window, sort of a pastoral, chewing-the-cud kind of view.

George borrows a horse trailer to pick up the cows he has bought. He and our neighbor Dan arrive with four cows in the trailer, driving it through the gate into the fenced pasture. I stand on our lawn, as far as I can be from the cows while still looking as if I'm a supportive wife. Dan lifts the bar on the trailer door and four cows come hurtling out, sprinting for the farthest part of the pasture.

George says, "You stay here and watch the cows. We have to go pick up four more." Before I can respond, Dan and George have already driven away. Alone with the cows, I dutifully watch them. What, exactly, am I supposed to watch them do? Break through the thin electrified fence? What do I do if that happens? They run amazingly fast, testing the perimeter, in a hyper-kinetic mass. This is not the pastoral scene I had imagined.

Dan's daughter—twenty-four and raised around livestock—joins us when Dan and George bring the next load of cows. I try to look calm and knowing. She says, "Isn't it weird how cows always get along and never bite each other to establish dominance like horses do?" Before she finishes her sentence, Dan opens the trailer door and 4,800 pounds of beef barrels out. The largest, a tawny cow, runs full speed toward our black and white boss cow across the field and rams her, skull to skull. With a loud cracking sound, the unsuspecting cow collapses to the ground. I think she's dead. Our jaws collectively hang open, stunned at the aggressive behavior. The downed cow slowly gets up, shakes her head and dazedly looks around. The new boss cow has clearly established herself. She turns to chew on some grass.

After a long summer with the herd, things have settled enough that we plan a weekend away. I'm still getting used to being in a field with Mini Cooper-sized animals, and I mentally wish our cow-sitter luck. I glance at the detailed instructions George leaves.

> The electric fence around the pasture and cross fencing is $#%)&!!^% "hot." If you need to turn off the fence, there are two yellow switches on the west gate—near the asparagus patch. One controls all of the fencing. The second controls the fence along the stack of irrigation pipe to the west. *Are you with me so far?* Always CLOSE THE GATE behind you. Even if it is to part of the pasture where the animals are not presently grazing.

Shortly into our weekend, we receive a text from our house sitter: "The truck died so I left it in the field. Sleeting rain. Don't worry ... cows are fed."

OK. We can fix the truck when we get home.

Early next morning, a second text, "Woke to sound of mooing near bedroom. Forgot to close the gate. How to get cows back in field?"

With a heavy sigh, George texts, "Load hay bales into wheelbarrow. Loudly and continuously call out 'mmm-bows' while leading cows into field. Then CLOSE THE GATE."

Because we'll sell the cows at auction or slaughter them for beef, we don't name them. This creates some interesting interactions.

One day George calls the vet because one of the mamas stopped eating. As George describes the symptoms, the receptionist interrupts, "What is the name of your animal?"

George hesitates, "Umm, White-Faced Mama." After a long pause on the other end of the phone, "What type of animal is that?"

"A cow," George replies.

We don't own a bull because they can wreak havoc on fencing. We agree to barter our hay for breeding services with our neighbor's bull, Patrick, who has been trained to come to the smell of bread. Patrick—a massive bull at 2,600 pounds—will walk right up to you, wanting his head scratched while he curls his long, black tongue around slices of bread.

Patrick lets us know when it's time to visit our cow ladies by pacing along our shared fence line, emitting a deep bass thrumming that haunts our bedroom at night. From a *basso profundo*, he works into the upper register of a high-pitched bugling elk. When we open the gate between our two pastures, Patrick moves purposefully into the field. He finds a dry patch of ground and paws at it to work up some good dust. Headfirst he bends into the dirt and swings his head back and forth to ensure full coverage. Then he raises his head as if to say, "How do I look, ladies?"

This is good farm entertainment. With his love paint on, Patrick sidles up to the lady cow of his choice and sniffs her. They stand side by side for a while and eat grass. He rests his box-shaped head and thick neck on her comparatively slender neck. And then a few other things happen and that's how calves are made.

This summer, we keep the back pasture closed so the grass can regenerate. We wait impatiently for the rain to start. When we finally open the gate to allow grazing, the cows come running clear across the field, kicking up their back legs like it's the last day of school, giddy with the scent of new grass.

I have learned many important lessons from the herd:

1. Cows are curious.

2. The boss cow will respond to a call of "mmm-bows" and the herd will follow.

3. When cows are moved into a corral and sense something bad is going to happen, they can jump a six-foot-high gate, land on their head and do a somersault.

4. When castrating calves, reach in from the side to avoid getting kicked.

5. Holding a distressed newborn calf upside down and thumping its chest will cause it to start breathing.

6. Make sure your thumb stays out of the way of the needle when vaccinating calves.

7. Never underestimate how fast cows can run.

8. Hefting sixty-five-pound bales of hay builds strong lats.

9. Do not allow husband to attend his fiftieth high school reunion in Philadelphia during calving season.

10. Keep a close eye on the reading material by husband's bedside.

What the Road Reveals

The answer must be, I think, that beauty and grace are performed whether or not we will or sense them. The least we can do is try and be there.
—Annie Dillard

Turning onto the road that leads to our farm, a flash of periwinkle catches my eye. A ring-necked duck in breeding plumage with his gray-blue bill paddles alone in the creek, clearly looking for love. Further down the creek, I spot the glossy emerald head and bright orange bill of a wood duck. I hope they aren't competing for territory.

A doe with her sweet twins uses our road as a byway of sorts. They bed down near the creek and I often see them crossing our road northbound toward the river swale where they forage for breakfast. Mom crosses first, handily clearing the six-foot-high pasture fence. The twins follow by scooting under the lowest strand of barbed wire.

One early morning I turn onto the road from the street and pull up sharp to accommodate a slow, waddling skunk. I follow, allowing for a safe distance between the two of us so he doesn't startle and spray.

A few months back, I would have missed this. Before I retired as CEO of a regional nonprofit, my time on our road consisted of heading to work early in the morning, in the dark, and coming home after work, in the dark. I mentally donned alligator skin each morning to toughen myself for the relentless attacks against the nonprofit's mission and morals. I was impatient with everything and everyone that got in my way of keeping the organization strong.

This single-minded focus created a lot of stress in my body. The physical therapist I'm seeing to unlock this tension is manipulating my fascia to create room. The farm chores that now govern my schedule, which often involve lifting heavy objects, make me more deliberate about the mechanics of how I move. Counter-intuitively, this deceleration creates time. When the alligator skin begins to slough off and I can feel myself soften, my awareness grows.

Traveling the road in daylight hours generates a newfound sense of wonder and appreciation for the creatures who share this space. When I slow down and pay attention, when I'm no longer jumping ahead to the day's frenetic meeting schedule, when my thoughts are not consumed by personnel issues and budget shortages, I am rewarded with glimpses of the wild.

Our access road is a half-mile long and curved, so you can't see the end from the beginning. It matches the meander of the adjacent creek that forms its southern border. More than sixty-one inches of rain have already fallen in our "rain year" that extends October through April—the wettest in history. The creek has been just below flood stage for weeks. I spot our resident beaver, who makes his home along the bank, hunkered down in the pasture. Is he feeding? Waterlogged? Injured? Some days his commute across the road coincides with mine and I wait patiently for him to cross. He has a bit of a limp, so it's slow going. I don't mind.

In early February, my feelings for the beaver were not so sublime. S/he was busily falling trees to construct a dam and the cottonwoods kept landing across our road rather than in the creek. I worried this would continue until every tree had been downed, decimating our riparian border. Three mornings in a row the fallen trees required backing up my car toward the house to wake my husband so he could use the chain saw to clear the road. I received my own (smaller, lighter) chain saw on Valentine's Day, so I could clear the road myself. I kept boots and saw in the trunk of my car for weeks until the beaver's home was finished.

The heavy rain has ravaged our road—a series of deep gouges need filling. We hope two yards of gravel might be enough. On the first dry day, we load the pickup truck so full that its nose points to heaven and the tailgate slopes dangerously downward. I drive along our easement and my husband walks behind me shoveling gravel into the holes. With a pace of about three miles an hour, I have plenty of time to look around. The yellow-orange stiletto bill of a great egret pokes down into the grassy shallows at creek's edge, spearing lunch. We scare up a family of California quail who go nattering alongside, outrunning the truck.

Three weeks ago my husband spied a fox standing quietly where the road empties onto the main street. Its fur was more gray blue than the tawny-reddish female we've seen in past years. Since this sighting I have been sending out fox vibes, hoping to be as lucky.

Observing wild lives parallel to our own transforms the mundane errands on the road into joyful surprises and shifts my sense of place, opening a portal into another realm. When the Canada goose pair honks into view, circling in wide arcs, I stop the car and crane my neck to witness a bombardier-like landing in the top of the cottonwood snag. One stations itself as lookout while the other lands smoothly on the water. They engage in a honking call and response as though reassuring each other.

A day when the sun is high overhead, I walk to the end of the road to fetch the mail. Turkey vultures circle lazily above me, spiraling in toward their roosting tree. Three of them land near the top of the tree as though it's afternoon break time.

My enchantment at these sightings spills over and I can't wait to tell my husband. Keeping curious makes me aware that there is so much going on outside my own self-obsessed, zooming, yammering, monkey mind. If I pay attention, my soul is nourished. If I remember to inhale with my eyes and ears, as well as my nose, the road reveals what has been in plain sight all along.

gratitude

I thank fellow writers Tom Titus, Evelyn Searle Hess, Kirsten Steen, Kay Porter, Cliff Scovall, Yvonne Young, Celeste Rose and Charleyne Gates—members of Red Moons writing critique group all—for their helpful counsel on many of the chapters.

Deep gratitude to Bob Welch, who accepted my first essay for the now-defunct Write On column in the *Register-Guard* in Eugene; and to Guy Maynard, now-retired editor of the *Oregon Quarterly*, for publishing my essay on rowing for the Oregon Trails feature. Their early encouragement kept me writing.

Early mentors John Daniel and Elizabeth Lyon both provided excellent critique and guidance to me when I was a member of their writing groups.

Kudos to Suzi Prozanski for her editorial assistance with my flabby verbs.

Thanks to Sherri Van Ravenhorst for her patience in designing various book covers even as I kept changing the name of the book.

Appreciation to early readers Eileen Klingaman and Amy Smucker for their helpful recommendations. All errors are mine alone.

Bouquets to my stepsons, Nat and Josh, my sister Sallie, and many dear friends, who fill my life with joy and love, and unknowingly provided fodder for these stories—surprise!

I am indebted to my parents, Sharold and Patricia, who taught me so much about how to live my life. What resilient role models to have in this world.

Enormous love to my husband, George, for sharing this homespun life.

www.ingramcontent.com/pod-product-compliance
Lightning Source LLC
Chambersburg PA
CBHW032209040426
42449CB00005B/503